ZOOM In on Animals!

Kangaroos
Up Close

Carmen Bredeson

Enslow Elementary

CONTENTS

WORDS TO KNOW

balance (BA luns)—To stay steady and not tip over.

dingoes (DING gohz)—Wild dogs that live in Australia.

joey (JOH ee)—A baby kangaroo.

pouch (POWCH)—A bag used to hold something.

Parts of a Kangaroo

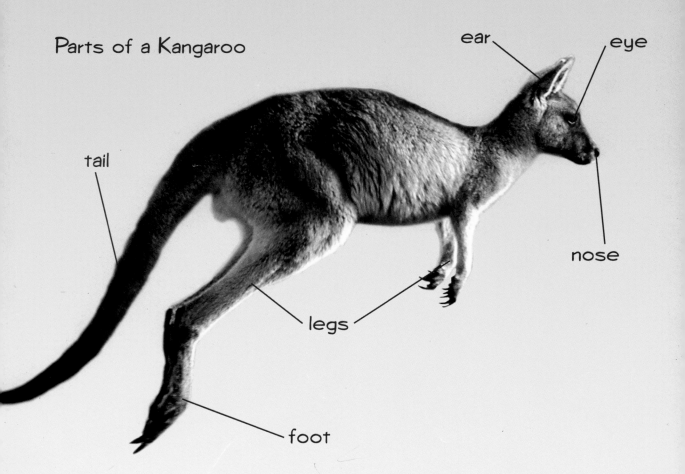

KANGAROO HOMES

Australia is home to most kangaroos. They live in forests and dry grasslands. Kangaroos spend the hot part of the day resting in the shade. They eat at night when it is cooler.

Australia

KANGAROO LEGS

UP CLOSE

Kangaroos do not walk like most animals. A kangaroo's front legs are very short. Its back legs are like springs. Kangaroos HOP, HOP, HOP to move from place to place. They can hop for a long way to look for food.

KANGAROO FEET

front foot

back foot

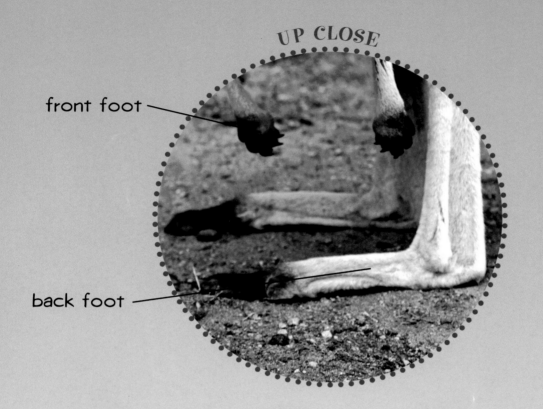

A kangaroo's back feet are BIG! One toe on each back foot is sharp like a knife. These toes are used for fighting. The front feet are small. Sometimes kangaroos clean their fur with their front feet.

KANGAROO TAIL

A kangaroo's big, strong tail is nearly as long as its body. The tail helps the kangaroo keep its **balance** when it is hopping. A kangaroo rests on its tail when it is sitting.

KANGAROO TEETH

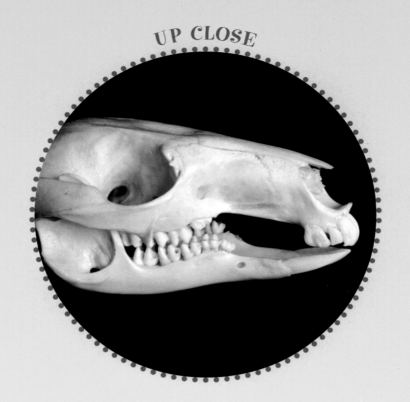

Kangaroos eat grass and plants. Big front teeth cut the plants near the ground. Then the back teeth grind up the plants. Kangaroos get most of the water they need from the plants they eat.

KANGAROO FUR

UP CLOSE

Some kangaroos have red fur. Others have gray or brown fur. A kangaroo's fur is soft and wooly. Kangaroos lick their fur. This helps the animals stay cool. It also keeps their fur clean.

KANGAROO EARS

UP CLOSE

Kangaroos can turn their ears different ways. The ears help them hear where danger is coming from. **Dingoes** hunt and kill kangaroos. Cars, trucks, and hunters can kill them too.

dingo

KANGAROO JOEY

A baby kangaroo is called a **joey**. It is the size of a jelly bean when it is born. The tiny baby crawls into its mother's **pouch** and drinks milk.

KANGAROO POUCH

A kangaroo's pouch is like a big pocket.
A joey spends seven or eight months in its
mother's pouch. Then it leaves the pouch,
but stays near its mother. If danger is near,
the joey hops right back into the safe pouch.

LIFE CYCLE

A newborn is the size of a jelly bean.

The joey leaves the pouch after seven or eight months.

Adult kangaroos can live to be twenty years old.

LEARN MORE

BOOKS

Ripple, William John. *Kangaroos*. Mankato, Minn.: Pebble Books, 2005.

Sill, Cathryn P., and John Sill. *About Marsupials: A Guide for Children*. Atlanta: Peachtree, 2006.

Spilsbury, Louise, and Richard Spilsbury. *Watching Kangaroos in Australia*. Chicago: Heinemann Library, 2006.

WEB SITES

Animal Planet: Australia Zoo
<http://animal.discovery.com/fansites/crochunter/australiazoo/australiazoo.html>

Creature World
<http://www.pbs.org/kratts/world/aust/kangaroo/>

National Geographic Coloring Book
<http://www.nationalgeographic.com/coloringbook/kangaroos.html>

INDEX

Series Literacy Consultant:
Allan A. De Fina, Ph.D.
Past President of the New Jersey Reading Association
Chairperson, Department of Literacy Education
New Jersey City University
Jersey City, New Jersey

Science Consultant:
Patrick Thomas, Ph.D.
General Curator
Bronx Zoo
Wildlife Conservation Society
Bronx, New York

Note to Parents and Teachers: The **Zoom In on Animals!** series supports the National Science Education Standards for K–4 science. The Words to Know section introduces subject-specific vocabulary words, including pronunciation and definitions. Early readers may need help with these new words.

Enslow Elementary, an imprint of Enslow Publishers, Inc.

Enslow Elementary® is a registered trademark of Enslow Publishers, Inc.

Copyright © 2009 by Carmen Bredeson

Library of Congress Cataloging-in-Publication Data

Bredeson, Carmen.
    Kangaroos up close / Carmen Bredeson.
        p. cm. — (Zoom in on animals!)
    Summary: "Provides an up-close look at kangaroos for new readers"—Provided by publisher.
    Includes bibliographical references and index.
    ISBN-13: 978-0-7660-3079-4
    ISBN-10: 0-7660-3079-2
    1. Kangaroos—Juvenile literature. I. Title.
    QL737.M35B74 2008
    599.2'22—dc22   2007034799

Printed in the United States of America

10 9 8 7 6 5 4 3 2 1

To Our Readers: We have done our best to make sure all Internet Addresses in this book were active and appropriate when we went to press. However, the author and the publisher have no control over and assume no liability for the material available on those Internet sites or on other Web sites they may link to. Any comments or suggestions can be sent by e-mail to comments@enslow.com or to the address on the back cover.

♻ Enslow Publishers, Inc., is committed to printing our books on recycled paper. The paper in every book contains 10% to 30% post-consumer waste (PCW). The cover board on the outside of each book contains 100% PCW. Our goal is to do our part to help young people and the environment too!

Photo Credits: © 1999, Artville, LLC, p. 5; © 2007 Jupiterimages Corporation, p. 17 (inset); Alamy: © Dave Watts, pp. 10, 15; © JTB Photo Communications, Inc., p. 11; © Slick Shoots; p. 8; © Alan Root/OSF/Animals Animals, pp. 18, 22 (top left); Artville, p. 5 (map); © Enzo & Paolo Ragazzini/CORBIS, p. 12; Dave Watts/Tom Stack & Associates, pp. 3, 4–5, 7; Howie Garber/Getty Images, p. 19; iStockphoto.com: © Alan Hewitt, p. 16; © Sylvia Smart, p. 6; © Jean Paul Ferrero/ardea.com, p. 9; © NHPA/Martin Harvey, p. 13; Shutterstock, pp. 1, 14, 22 (bottom); © SuperStock, Inc., pp. 20, 22 (top right); © Theo Allofs/Visuals Unlimited, p. 17; William D. Bachman/Photo Researchers, Inc., p. 21.

Front Cover Photos: © Alan Hewitt/iStockphoto.com (left); © Theo Allofs/Visuals Unlimited (top right, center right); William D. Bachman/Photo Researchers, Inc. (bottom right).

Back Cover Photo: William D. Bachman/Photo Researchers, Inc.

Enslow Elementary
an imprint of
Enslow Publishers, Inc.
40 Industrial Road
Box 398
Berkeley Heights, NJ 07922
USA
http://www.enslow.com